miles davis
BIRTH OF THE COOL

ISBN 0-634-00682-7

HAL•LEONARD®
CORPORATION

7777 W. BLUEMOUND RD. P.O. BOX 13819 MILWAUKEE, WI 53213

Visit Hal Leonard Online at
www.halleonard.com

miles davis
BIRTH OF THE COOL

"Birth of the Cool Theme" was broadcast from the Royal Roost (1580 Broadway, New York City) over WMCA (570 AM) and recorded off the air by Boris Rose. "Joost at the Roost" was never recorded by the nonet. The remaining titles were recorded at Capitol Records' New York studio at 151 West 46th Street.

Introduction

This landmark publication presents the music of the Miles Davis Nonet in concert score format, restored from as many of the original parts as still exist. In preparation for over two years, this publication is as definitive as is possible given that only one manuscript score exists at this writing, and individual parts are missing on some titles. But for the first time, these pieces are available in one publication, drawn from the composer/arrangers' own autograph parts.

The story of this folio begins in Gil Evans' single-room apartment at 14 West 55th Street in 1946. The new music called bebop was taking the jazz world by storm, and the clubs on 52nd Street were filled with musicians and fans supporting the music. At that time, Evans was de facto musical director of the Claude Thornhill Orchestra, writing innovative, challenging music for a unique dance band that included French horns and tuba. Evans' apartment became a hangout for musicians, who knew that the door would always be unlocked and they were welcome anytime, even if Evans wasn't home. It was not uncommon for Gil to come home to find Charlie Parker asleep while a couple of other musicians listened to recordings and studied scores of Prokofiev symphonies. Several musicians down on their luck moved in for indeterminate periods, and the apartment was a meeting ground for younger arrangers in search of encouragement and direction. Gil was the older, experienced, successful professional whom they looked up to and learned from. In turn, Gil enjoyed their company and their new ideas. He hadn't had much of a formal musical education, and he welcomed the "bull sessions" that never stopped.

By mid-1947, Evans was interested in furthering the bebop aspects of the Thornhill book, and Thornhill was just as anxious for the band to remain an ensemble specializing in ballads. Evans began sketching out ideas for a smaller-sized ensemble that duplicated the coloristic properties of the Thornhill band. By early 1948, discussions about such an ensemble began with Evans, John Carisi, John Lewis, Johnny Mandel, Gerry Mulligan, and George Russell, the nucleus of those who were interested in writing for such a group. Carisi had played in the Glenn Miller Army Air Force Band and participated in jam sessions of the new music in 1944. Lewis was working as a pianist on 52nd Street and was writing for the Dizzy Gillespie band. Mandel had played and written for Boyd Raeburn and Buddy Rich. Mulligan had written for Gene Krupa and Thornhill. Russell had played drums with the

Benny Carter band, and was already formulating what would become his groundbreaking and influential Lydian Chromatic Concept.

According to Carisi, the instrumentation was decided based on treble and bass components of like instruments; alto and baritone saxophones, trumpet and trombone, French horn and tuba. It was Miles Davis who made the group a reality. Mulligan has stated that Miles' sound and approach appealed to all the writers, and once Miles joined in the discussions at Gil's apartment, he took the project over, alerting other musicians to join and calling rehearsals. Although the personnel of the group was never locked in, the best musicians in New York were invited to participate (by this time, Mandel had left New York to establish his residency with Local 47 of the American Federation of Musicians in Los Angeles). The group began rehearsals at Nola Studios during the summer of 1948, and as good as the players were, there were many breakdowns while rehearsing the music; often the arrangers had to sing the parts the way they wanted them played. Even though there were any number of rehearsal bands in New York in 1948, the music for this group was like no other written up to that time. Lewis, Carisi, Mulligan, Russell, and Evans regarded this ensemble as an experimental arrangers band where they could try things out and learn. Mulligan experimented with time changes and counterpoint, Carisi wrote a blues with complex chordal voicings and counterpoint.

During this time, Miles was performing with Charlie Parker, and was playing with various ensembles at the Royal Roost. He convinced owner Monte Kay to book the unorthodox nonet. The group played two alternating weeks at the club during September of 1948, the first week sharing the bandstand with the Count Basie Orchestra. Ten selections from two broadcasts emceed by "Symphony Sid" Torin over WMCA were bootlegged until they were issued legally on Capitol Records in 1998. The arrangers' names were prominently displayed on a billboard outside the club. Reaction to the band was mixed, not only because of its unusual style, but based on the broadcasts, many of the performances were ragged. However, the music caught the attention of Pete Rugolo, New York musical director of Capitol Records and an innovative composer himself, and Walter Rivers, a Capitol employee who was founder Johnny Mercer's cousin. Rugolo signed the band to record twelve sides, and two sessions took place in 1949 (January 21 and April 22) and one in

1950 (March 9). Sonically, the recordings have a wide range and great clarity (they were among the earliest recordings made using magnetic tape instead of lacquer master discs), but the instrumentation was so unique that the recording engineers were never able to get a good sound balance for the group.

Ironically, by the time of the second session, the nonet had played one more gig and had effectively disbanded. One final appearance took place for one night at Birdland sometime in late March of 1950 (where the pianist was none other than Bud Powell), but all of the musicians were involved with other projects by then. Capitol only released a few of the sides; they received little attention from the press and sold poorly (however, according to Rugolo, none of Capitol's modern jazz recordings were promoted properly and all of them suffered poor sales). Since only a few sides were released at the time, there was nothing to suggest that something different and unusual had taken place in American music. Perhaps no one outside of New York thought of this group as a potentially working band, and treated these sides as if Miles was backed by a studio ensemble assembled just for recordings.

In 1954, Rugolo persuaded Capitol to release eight of the twelve sides on a 10" Capitol album called *Classics in Jazz – Miles Davis*. In 1957, eleven of the tracks were issued on a 12" album entitled *The Birth of the Cool*, the first time the famous phrase was coined describing the ensemble and its music. It was long assumed that producer Rugolo was responsible for the title, but he has denied this.

What took place was the long overdue recognition for the ensemble and its music, heard by most American and European musicians for the first time. Both positive and negative articles about the music appeared around the world, but arrangers and composers such as Shorty Rogers, Jack Montrose, Andre Hodeir, Andre Previn, Henry Mancini, and many others were influenced by it. These recordings as a group eventually became as influential as the Louis Armstrong Hot Fives and Sevens, the 1940-42 recordings by the Duke Ellington Orchestra, and the Dizzy Gillespie-Charlie Parker small group sides. They have never been out of print since 1957, and have been digitally remastered as recently as 2001.

The Composer/Arrangers
GIL EVANS
Evans was born in Canada in 1912. Primarily self-taught, he led an excellent territory big band in Southern California during the thirties. The ensemble was eventually sold to singer Skinnay Ennis in 1938, and Gil continued to arrange for the band. He met pianist/arranger Claude Thornhill at this time,

who became the musical director of the Ennis band. In 1941, Thornhill started his own ensemble and took Evans with him as arranger in 1941. Thornhill joined the Navy during the war, and reorganized in 1946. This postwar unit stands out as one of the most innovative ensembles of all time, featuring Evans' arrangements of modern jazz classics such as "Donna Lee," "Anthropology," and "Yardbird Suite." After his work with the Miles Davis Nonet, Evans seemingly disappeared, playing piano in bars and writing for singers. It was the album *Miles Ahead*, one of the first albums as part of Miles' new contract with Columbia Records, which restored Evans to his rightful place as an innovator and great musical thinker. Other albums with Davis such as *Porgy and Bess* and *Sketches of Spain* were best-sellers, which have never gone out of print.

Evans later put together a band of his own in 1960, and wrote and conducted a series of excellent albums for Verve, which were produced by Creed Taylor. Evans and Miles last appeared at the 1968 Monterey Jazz Festival performing music from their various albums together. The concert was taped and hopefully will be released to the public.

In 1970, Evans reappeared with a new orchestra reflecting his interests in electronics and rock. Many fans were upset with his new musical direction, but he was determined to play the popular music of the time. His band was particularly popular at European jazz festivals. A folio of his music was published by Hal Leonard Corporation (HL00672327) which includes music from his Thornhill work through to his last band. He died in 1988. Gil's son Miles continues to lead the Gil Evans Orchestra.

JOHN LEWIS
Born in Illinois, Lewis studied anthropology and music at the University of New Mexico. After military service, his piano skills quickly established him in the modern jazz world. Lewis replaced Thelonious Monk in the Dizzy Gillespie big band. He was all over 52nd Street, playing and recording with Charlie Parker, Illinois Jacquet, Ella Fitzgerald, and Lester Young during the period of the Davis nonet. In fact, it was a recording date with Fitzgerald that prevented Lewis from participating in the group's first recording date. Al Haig took his place.

In 1952, Lewis recorded in a quartet setting with Milt Jackson, Percy Heath, and Kenny Clarke. This unit, with Connie Kaye substituting for Clarke, later became the Modern Jazz Quartet. Lewis was its musical director and wrote many acclaimed compositions for the ensemble, which stayed together until 1974. Lewis was also involved with symphonic music utilizing jazz elements, called "Third Stream." The MJQ re-formed in 1981, and in between world tours, Lewis recorded as a pianist and taught at City University of New York and Harvard. He died in 2001.

GERRY MULLIGAN

In 1948 Gerry Mulligan was already established as one of the most promising composer/arrangers of the era; his music for the Gene Krupa orchestra attracted great attention in the jazz world. Mulligan's "Disk Jockey Jump" was a hit record for Krupa in 1946, and Gerry's treatments of such classic songs as "If You Were the Only Girl in the World" showed his maturity in harmony and counterpoint. It was Gil Evans who convinced him to relocate to New York from Philadelphia, and Evans exposed him to modern classical music. Gil also got Mulligan arranging work with the Thornhill band; full band arrangements of "Jeru," "Godchild," and "Joost at the Roost" were written for Thornhill, and "Rock Salt" was part of the Elliot Lawrence library. Mulligan later said, "Gil wasn't the only influence on my writing–he was the final influence."

At this time, Mulligan was an adequate improviser at best, but he was practicing like crazy, subbing in big bands, and participating in every jam session that he could attend. Playing in the Miles Davis Nonet gave him solo opportunities, and even though his solos were tentative at this time, he already had a unique sound and style.

He recorded with his own nonet for Prestige in 1951, and soon afterward relocated to Los Angeles. An association writing for Stan Kenton was short-lived, but he soon had a regular Monday night gig at the Haig. He met trumpeter Chet Baker, and their intuitive rapport, coupled with the fact that the rhythm section did not include a piano, soon made the Mulligan/Baker quartet the hottest attraction in the area. Their recordings made them international stars.

The group disbanded when Mulligan was arrested for drug possession; he was released in 1954. Baker was now leading his own group, so Mulligan put together a quartet with Bob Brookmeyer on valve trombone, although Mulligan and Baker had a few reunions on record and in concert throughout the years. In 1955-56, Mulligan recorded three albums with a sextet that were well received, but he was leading a quartet again by 1957.

In 1960, Mulligan formed a big band that he called the Concert Jazz Band. Arrangements were supplied by Brookmeyer, John Carisi, Bill Finegan, George Russell, Bill Holman, Al Cohn, and a newcomer named Gary McFarland. The musicians included Brookmeyer, Zoot Sims, Clark Terry, Nick Travis, Gene Quill, and Mel Lewis. One of the Mulligan compositions in the book was none other than "Joost at the Roost," which was recorded for Verve but never issued. Considered one of the great big bands of all time, it broke up in 1964. After some years of playing with Dave Brubeck's quartet, Mulligan put together another big band to record an album called *Age of Steam*, reflecting his love of trains. He continued to appear across the globe with his own ensembles until his death in 1996. A career highlight was his composition "Entente for Baritone Saxophone and Orchestra," which he performed with symphony orchestras all over the world.

Along with Gil Evans, Gerry Mulligan was the main architect for the Miles Davis Nonet. In "Jeru," "Venus De Milo," "Godchild," and "Rock Salt," there are strikingly innovative touches in orchestration and counterpoint. "Jeru" and "Joost at the Roost" have some of the earliest experiments in time signature changes in jazz, handled with grace and musicality.

Mulligan has rarely been given credit for the considerable role he played in this ensemble. He even re-recorded this music in 1991 for an album called *Re-Birth of the Cool*. Miles Davis almost participated in this reunion, but Mulligan did not get the original parts from him; except for "Boplicity," "Israel," "Moon Dreams," and "Rouge," Mulligan had to rely on transcriptions.

JOHN CARISI

Born in Hasbrouck Heights, New Jersey in 1922, Carisi played trumpet with saxophonist Babe Russin in 1940. He was a member of the Glenn Miller AAF Orchestra for a short time in 1943, and participated in jam sessions of the music later called bebop in 1944. Carisi wrote "Israel" while he was studying with distinguished composer Stefan Wolpe; he also arranged for the Ray McKinley and Claude Thornhill bands during this period.

During the '50s, he wrote for radio, television, and recordings; unfortunately, an album for RCA made in 1956 for the Jazz Workshop series was not released at the time, but some tracks later appeared on CD. His composition "Springsville" was arranged by Gil Evans and recorded by Miles Davis for the album *Miles Ahead*.

His notable compositions in the '60s included "Angkor Wat," "Moon Taj," (both of which were recorded under Gil Evans' name for the Impulse label), and a saxophone quartet for the New York Saxophone Quartet. Carisi arranged "Israel" for the Mulligan Concert Jazz Band, and the new version was recorded on Verve Records. In 1969, Carisi taught composition and arranging at City University of New York and Queens College, where this writer studied with him. He continued to free-lance as a trumpet player until his death in New York in 1992.

"Israel" has proven to be one of the most influential compositions of its time, and has become a standard in the jazz repertory.

The Restoration of the Music

Since the late '50s, the repertoire of the Miles Davis Nonet has been among the most requested group of pieces for ensembles to play and composers to study. Miles Davis retained the parts for all titles recorded except for "Moon Dreams" and "Boplicity." Copies of the original parts of these two arrangements from Gil Evans were obtained by the distinguished composer/conductor/writer Gunther Schuller; the originals seem to have disappeared. Mr. Schuller deserves a great deal of credit for publishing "Israel," "Jeru," and "Rock Salt" through his own company, Margun Music. Of these three compositions, "Israel" came the closest to the original parts. The two Mulligan pieces were obviously transcriptions. Gerry Mulligan retained copies of most of the music he wrote and performed over the years; this collection is now housed at the Library of Congress. Until copies of the originals were discovered, the 1948-49 versions of "Jeru" and "Rock Salt" were missing from his library.

For years musicians asked Miles to re-explore this repertoire in recordings and concerts. Miles wasn't interested in reviewing his past and put this part of his career behind him. Requests to get copies of the music of the nonet were met with silence. If an ensemble wanted to play something from this particular library, they had to transcribe it. And many did—it is safe to say that these pieces have been transcribed about as often as a classic Fletcher Henderson or Duke Ellington arrangement. Hence, the versions of all but "Boplicity," "Israel," and "Moon Dreams" on the *Re-Birth of the Cool* were transcriptions.

Sometime in 1995, Miles Davis' effects stored in a warehouse in Philadelphia were delivered to his estate lawyer. Those effects included three boxes of music, which were sent to Joe Muccioli of King

Brand Music in New York to organize and evaluate. I was one of the first people to look through these boxes, and it is a day I will never forget. All of the scores that Gil Evans wrote for Miles' classic albums were there, as well as the session parts. While Joe and I sorted through the boxes, many of the original pencil-copied parts of the nonet library began turning up. All of the parts still existed for some pieces, and in others, enough parts were available to assemble versions that were relatively close to the originals. Additional arrangements which were never recorded or broadcast were also found in the three boxes of music. At least one composition could not be restored due to some missing parts and a poor sound source—John Lewis' "S'il Vous Plait." But one unexpected bonus was found: Gerry Mulligan's "Joost at the Roost." Since this is the only piece that was not recorded, there are chord slashes where the solos occurred. Comparing the nonet version to the big band arrangement Mulligan wrote for the Claude Thornhill Orchestra in 1948 facilitated the editing of "Joost at the Roost." As stated earlier, Mulligan later added this piece to the Concert Jazz Band's book. Bassist Bill Crow supplied the tempo; it was missing on all sources.

Special Thanks

The preparation of this folio would not have been possible without the permission of the Estate of Miles Davis (Shukat, Arrow, Hafer & Weber, L.L.P; in particular Peter S. Shukat, Esq. and Ivan A. Saperstein), and the Estate of Gerry Mulligan (Franca Mulligan, Cathie Phillips). Both estates allowed me to examine photocopies of the original parts and examine numerous other documents in the holdings of both estates so that I could prepare new scores of these pieces. David Joyner of Pacific Lutheran University in Tacoma, Washington supplied copies of original arrangements from the Claude Thornhill library, as well as invaluable information about Gerry Mulligan's contributions to this ensemble based on his interviews with Mulligan at the University of North Texas. Walter Van de Leur, Bill Kirchner, Richard Sudhalter, Terry Teachout, Andrew Homzy, and Mark Lopeman supplied valuable information and feedback. A special thank-you to Dan Morgenstern and the staff of the Institute of Jazz Studies at Rutgers University (Ed Berger, Vincent Pelote, Tad Hershorn, Ann Kuebler) for supplying numerous documents, additional encouragement, and good advice always.

Jeff Sultanof

MOVE

By DENZIL DE COSTA BEST

*When played live, the drums had a four-bar solo intro.

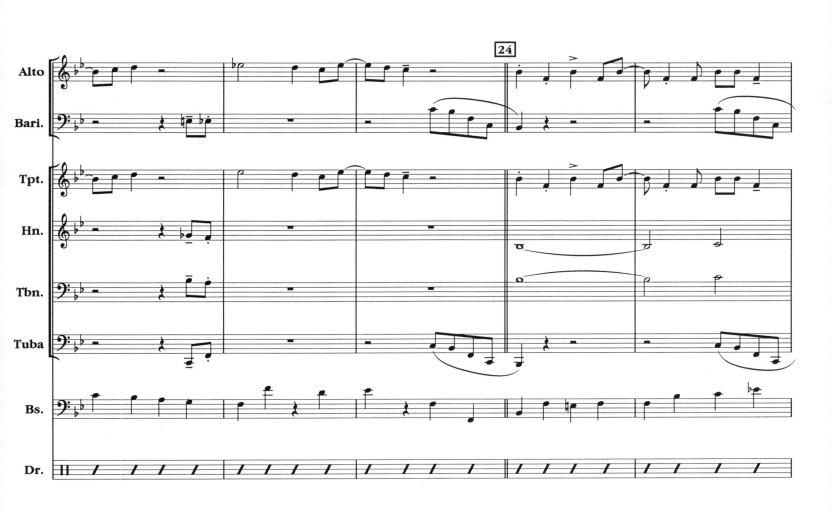

10

12

14

16

JERU

By GERRY MULLIGAN

22

*In the original parts Miles plays an additional 32-bar chorus with rhythm only.

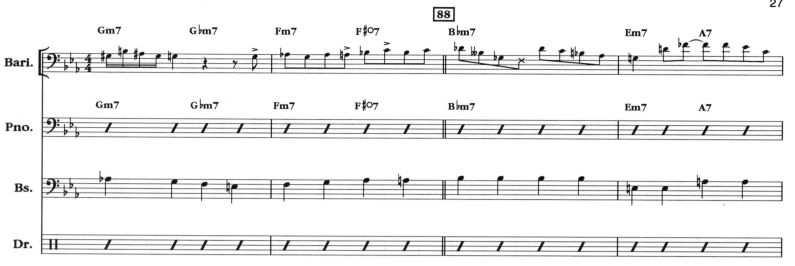

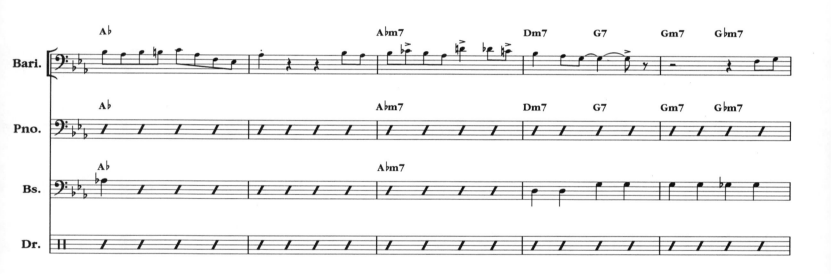

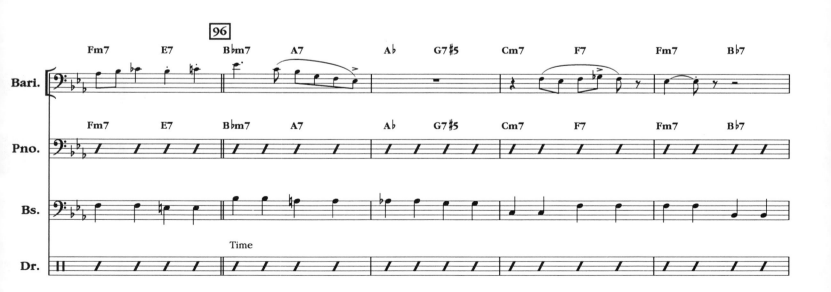

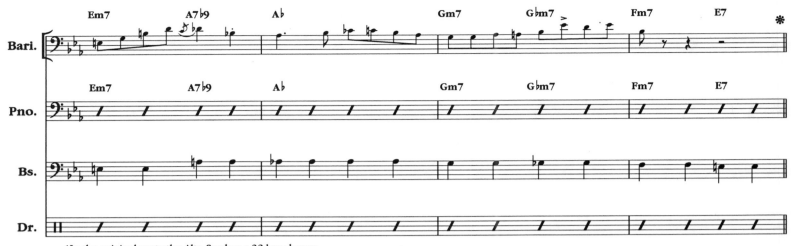

*In the original parts the Alto Sax has a 32 bar chorus
accompanied by rhythm only.

BUDO

By MILES DAVIS and BUD POWELL

36

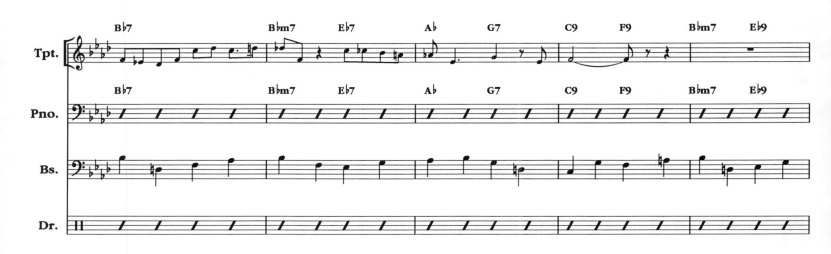

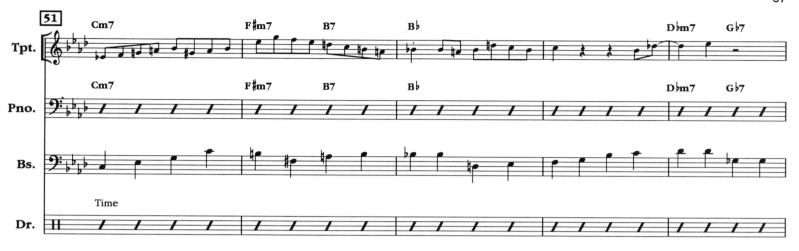

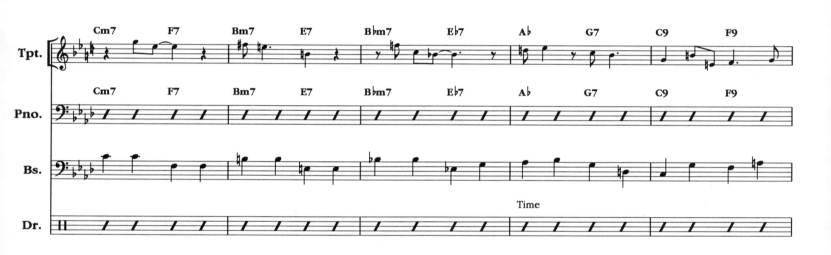

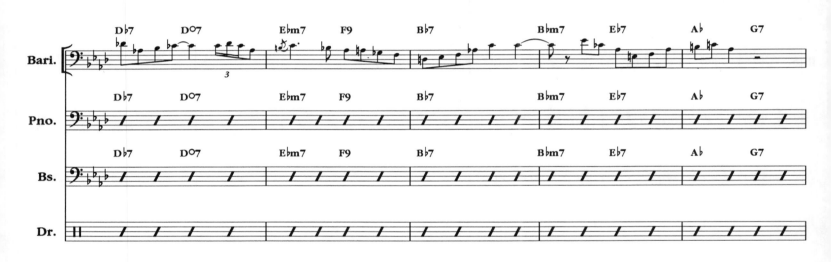

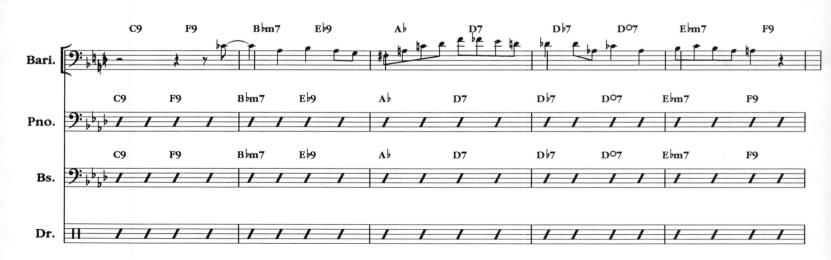

39

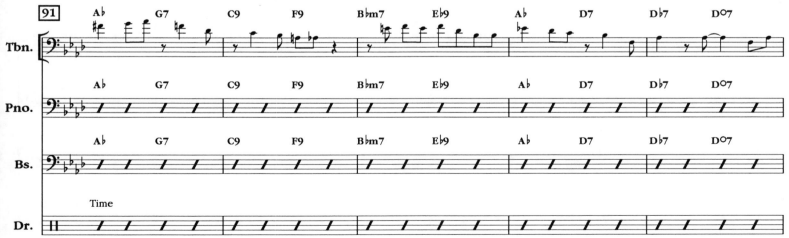

GODCHILD

Composed by GEORGE WALLINGTON

*Bars 5 - 15: even though this passage is in the original
part, it was not played. It is included here for
reference.

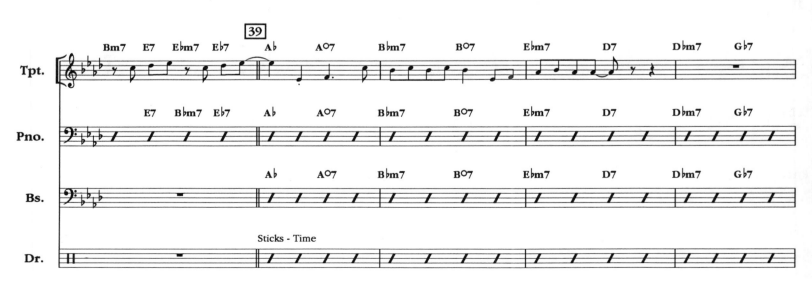

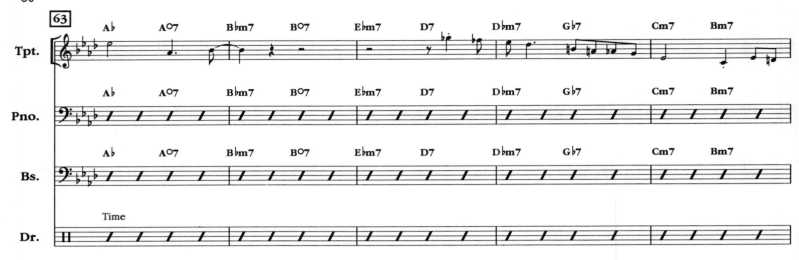

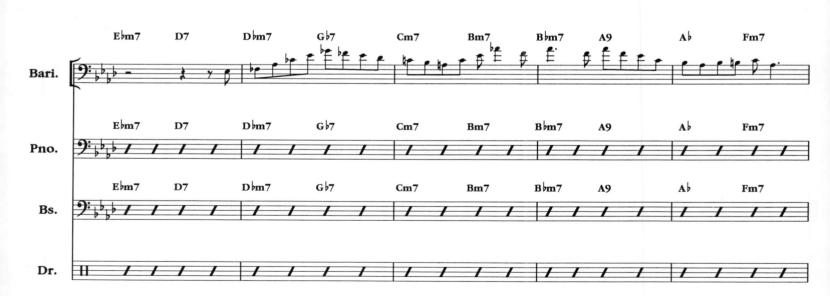

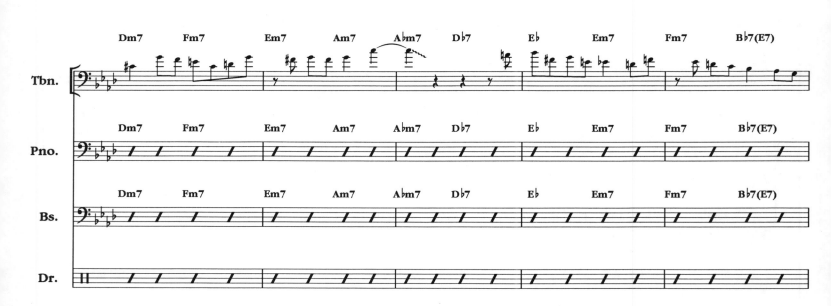

*This passage to the end is optional.

ISRAEL

By JOHN CARISI

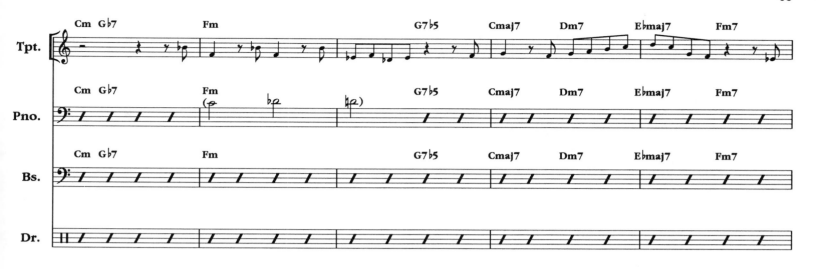

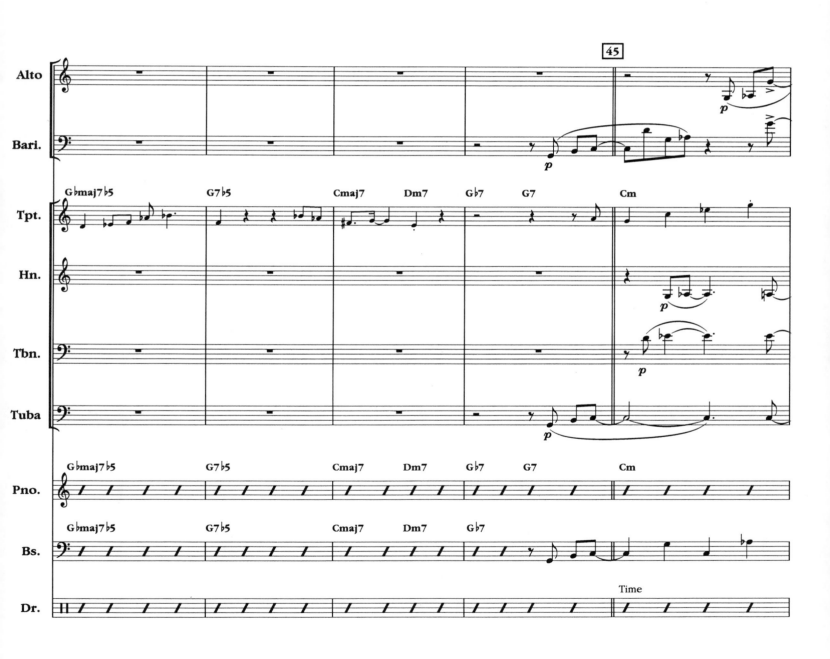

66

*On the recording, alto sax and rhythm section play these
three bars.

VENUS DE MILO

By GERRY MULLIGAN

*On original part "Hat" is indicated.

76

*This solo was cut from recording.

82

BOPLICITY
(BE BOP LIVES)

By MILES DAVIS

86

89

*This solo was written and appears in the part. Chord names are added for reference.

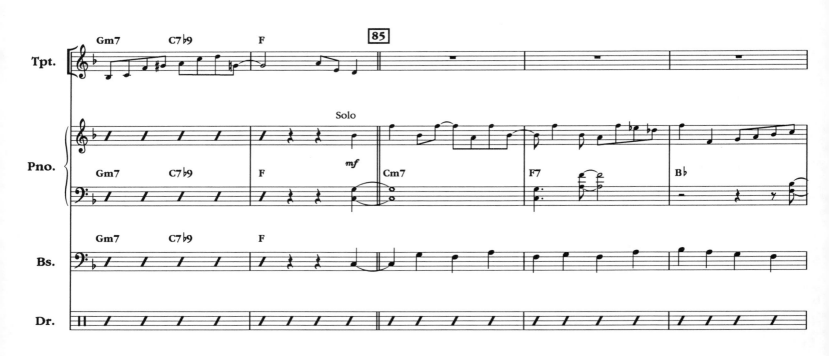

ROUGE

By JOHN LEWIS

Medium Tempo ♩ = 144

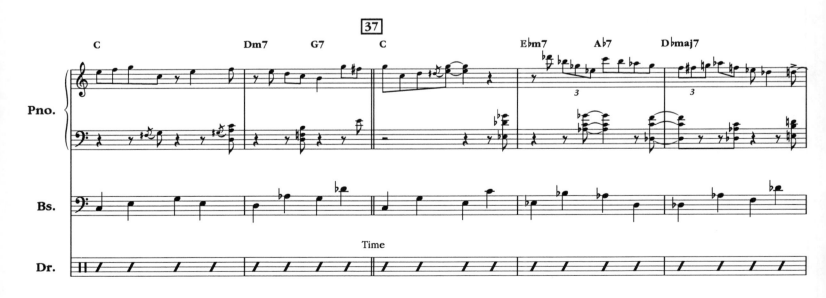

100

MOON DREAMS

Words and Music by CHUMMY MacGREGOR
and JOHNNY MERCER

Piano tacet throughout; the original chord names are
included for reference.

112

*These notes are in original part. Chord changes have
been added.

114

DECEPTION

By MILES DAVIS

*Miles's part has a variant of this melody, engraved as cue-size.

122

126

128

ROCK SALT
A/K/A ROCKER

By GERRY MULLIGAN

134

140

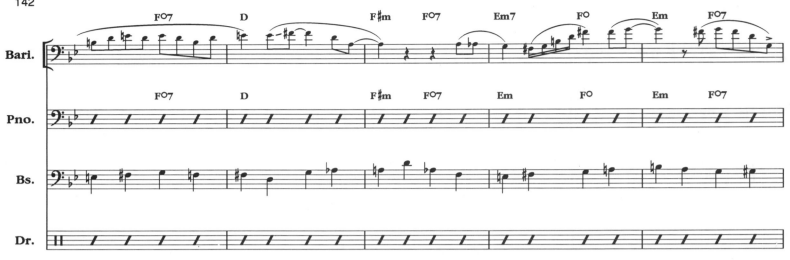

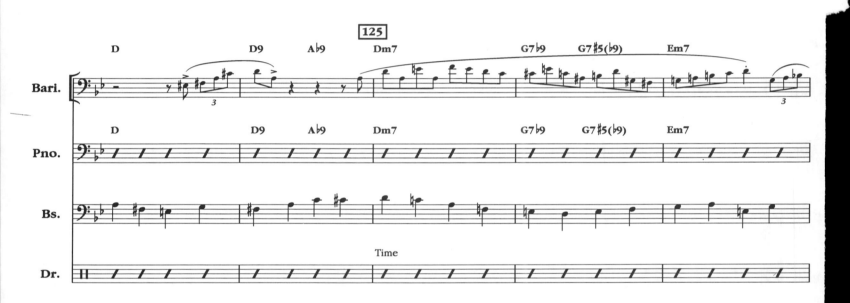

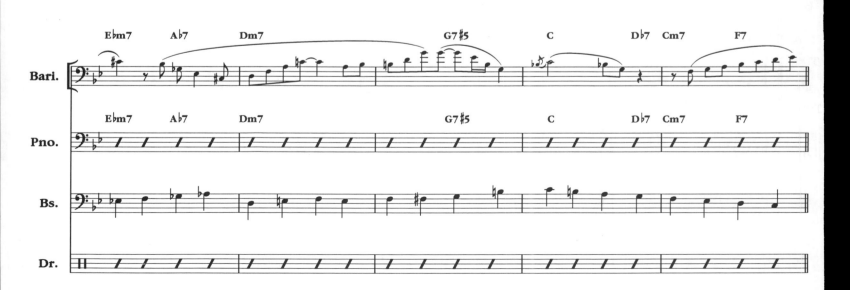

144

On the original parts, there is a repeat at 45 . The endings are reproduced here.

146

JOOST AT THE ROOST

By GERRY MULLIGAN

149

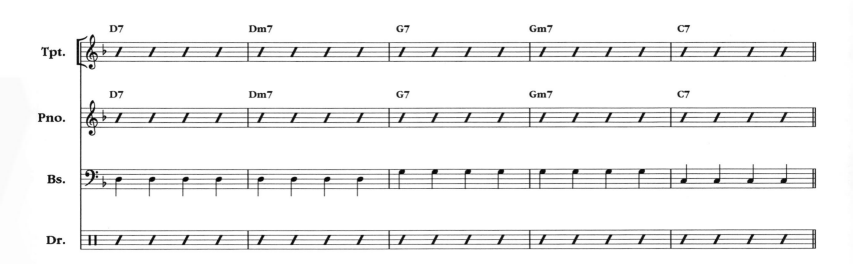

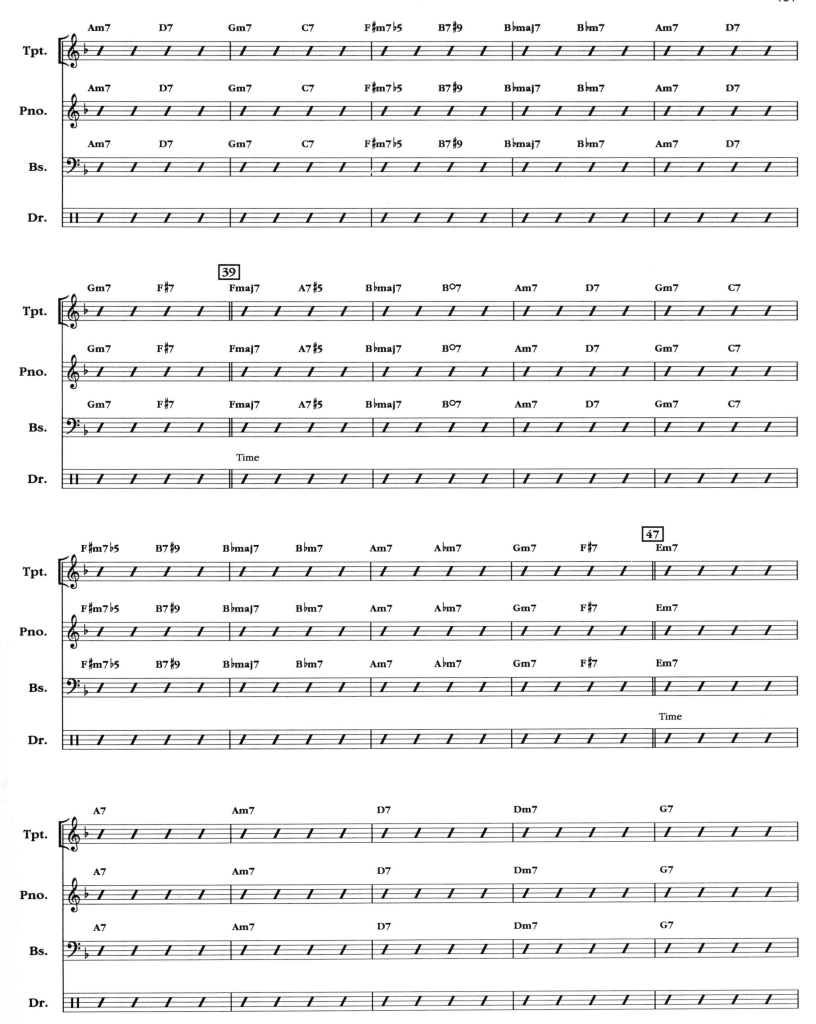

153

154

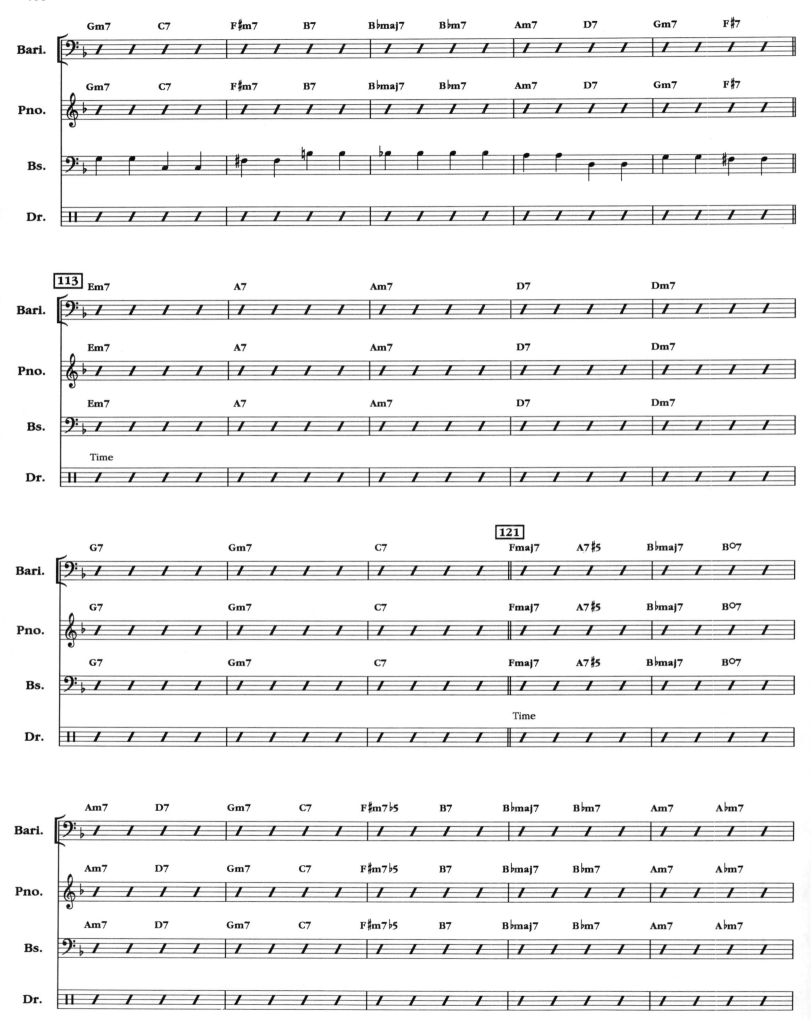

158

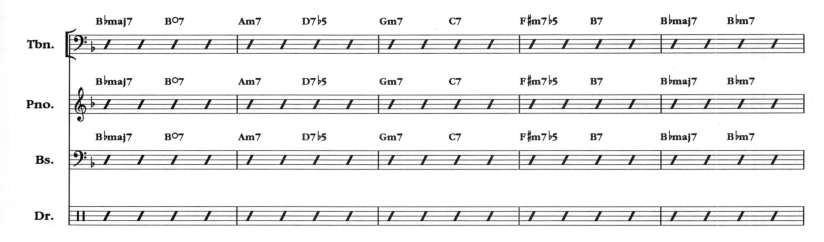

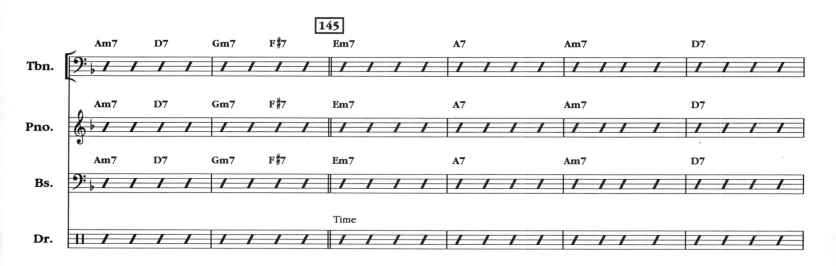

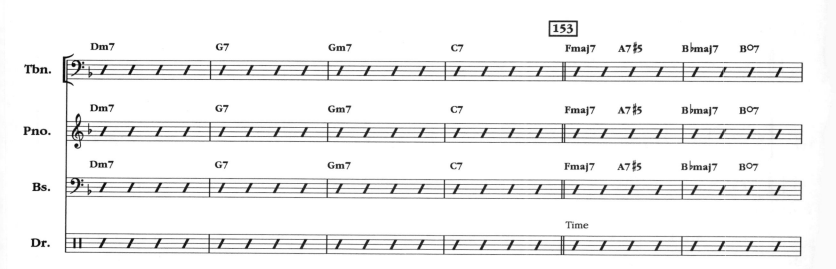

BIRTH OF THE COOL THEME

By GIL EVANS

ARTIST TRANSCRIPTIONS

Artist Transcriptions are authentic, note-for-note transcriptions of the hottest artists in jazz, pop, and rock today. These outstanding, accurate arrangements are in an easy-to-read format which includes all essential lines. Artist Transcriptions can be used to perform, sequence or reference.

GUITAR & BASS

The Guitar Style of George Benson
00660113 .... $14.95

The Guitar Book of Pierre Bensusan
00699072 .... $19.95

Ron Carter – Acoustic Bass
00672331 .... $16.95

**Charley Christian –
The Art of Jazz Guitar**
00026704 .... $9.95

Stanley Clarke Collection
00672307 .... $19.95

Al Di Meola – Cielo E Terra
00604041 .... $14.95

**Al Di Meola –
Friday Night in San Francisco**
00660115 .... $14.95

Al Di Meola – Music, Words, Pictures
00604043 .... $14.95

Kevin Eubanks Guitar Collection
00672319 .... $19.95

The Jazz Style of Tal Farlow
00673245 .... $19.95

Bela Fleck and the Flecktones
00672359 Melody/Lyrics/Chords $16.95

David Friesen – Years Through Time
00673253 .... $14.95

Best Of Frank Gambale
00672336 .... $22.95

Jim Hall – Jazz Guitar Environments
00699389 Book/CD $19.95

Jim Hall – Exploring Jazz Guitar
00699306 .... $17.95

Scott Henderson Guitar Book
00699330 .... $19.95

**Allan Holdsworth –
Reaching for the Uncommon Chord**
00604049 .... $14.95

Leo Kottke – Eight Songs
00699215 .... $14.95

Wes Montgomery – Guitar Transcriptions
00675536 .... $17.95

Joe Pass Collection
00672353 .... $18.95

John Patitucci
00673216 .... $14.95

Django Reinhardt Anthology
00027083 .... $14.95

The Genius of Django Reinhardt
00026711 .... $10.95

Django Reinhardt – A Treasury of Songs
00026715 .... $12.95

Great Rockabilly Guitar Solos
00692820 .... $14.95

Johnny Smith Guitar Solos
00672374 .... $16.95

Mike Stern Guitar Book
00673224 .... $16.95

Mark Whitfield
00672320 .... $19.95

Jack Wilkins – Windows
00673249 .... $14.95

Gary Willis Collection
00672337 .... $19.95

CLARINET

Buddy De Franco Collection
00672423 .... $19.95

TROMBONE

J.J. Johnson Collection
00672332 .... $19.95

TRUMPET

The Chet Baker Collection
00672435 .... $19.95

Randy Brecker
00673234 .... $14.95

**The Brecker Brothers...
And All Their Jazz**
00672351 .... $19.95

Best of the Brecker Brothers
00672447 .... $19.95

Miles Davis – Originals
00672448 .... $19.95

FLUTE

James Newton – Improvising Flute
00660108 .... $14.95

The Lew Tabackin Collection
00672455 .... $19.95

Miles Davis – Standards Vol. 1
00672450 .... $19.95

The Dizzy Gillespie Collection
00672479 .... $19.95

Freddie Hubbard
00673214 .... $14.95

Tom Harrell Jazz Trumpet
00672382 .... $19.95

Jazz Trumpet Solos
00672363 .... $9.95

PIANO & KEYBOARD

Monty Alexander Collection
00672338 .... $19.95

Kenny Barron Collection
00672318 .... $22.95

Warren Bernhardt Collection
00672364 .... $19.95

Cyrus Chesnut Collection
00672439 .... $19.95

Billy Childs Collection
00673242 .... $19.95

Chick Corea – Elektric Band
00603126 .... $15.95

Chick Corea – Paint the World
00672300 .... $12.95

Bill Evans Collection
00672365 .... $19.95

Benny Green Collection
00672329 .... $19.95

Herbie Hancock Collection
00672419 .... $19.95

Gene Harris Collection
00672446 .... $19.95

Ahmad Jamal Collection
00672322 .... $22.95

Jazz Master Classics for Piano
00672354 .... $14.95

**Thelonious Monk – Intermediate
Piano Solos**
00672392 .... $14.95

Jelly Roll Morton – The Piano Rolls
00672433 .... $12.95

Michel Petrucciani
00673226 .... $17.95

Bud Powell Classics
00672371 .... $19.95

André Previn Collection
00672437 .... $19.95

Horace Silver Collection
00672303 .... $19.95

Art Tatum Collection
00672316 .... $22.95

Art Tatum Solo Book
00672355 .... $19.95

Billy Taylor Collection
00672357 .... $24.95

McCoy Tyner
00673215 .... $16.95

Cedar Walton Collection
00672321 .... $19.95

SAXOPHONE

Julian "Cannonball" Adderly Collection
00673244 .... $18.95

Michael Brecker
00673237 .... $19.95

Michael Brecker Collection
00672429 .... $19.95

**The Brecker Brothers...
And All Their Jazz**
00672351 .... $19.95

Best of the Brecker Brothers
00672447 .... $19.95

Benny Carter Plays Standards
00672315 .... $22.95

Benny Carter Collection
00672314 .... $22.95

James Carter Collection
00672394 .... $19.95

John Coltrane – Giant Steps
00672349 .... $19.95

John Coltrane Solos
00673233 .... $22.95

Paul Desmond Collection
00672328 .... $19.95

Paul Desmond – Standard Time
00672454 .... $19.95

Stan Getz
00699375 .... $18.95

Stan Getz – Bossa Novas
00672377 .... $19.95

Stan Getz – Standards
00672375 .... $17.95

Great Tenor Sax Solos
00673254 .... $18.95

**Joe Henderson – Selections from
"Lush Life" & "So Near So Far"**
00673252 .... $19.95

Best of Joe Henderson
00672330 .... $22.95

Jazz Master Classics for Tenor Sax
00672350 .... $18.95

Best Of Kenny G
00673239 .... $19.95

Kenny G – Breathless
00673229 .... $19.95

Kenny G – Classics in the Key of G
00672462 .... $19.95

Kenny G – The Moment
00672373 .... $19.95

Joe Lovano Collection
00672326 .... $19.95

James Moody Collection – Sax and Flute
00672372 .... $19.95

The Frank Morgan Collection
00672416 .... $19.95

The Art Pepper Collection
00672301 .... $19.95

Sonny Rollins Collection
00672444 .... $19.95

David Sanborn Collection
00675000 .... $16.95

The Lew Tabackin Collection
00672455 .... $19.95

Stanley Turrentine Collection
00672334 .... $19.95

Ernie Watts Saxophone Collection
00673256 .... $18.95

FOR MORE INFORMATION, SEE YOUR LOCAL MUSIC DEALER,
OR WRITE TO:

HAL•LEONARD®
CORPORATION

7777 W. BLUEMOUND RD. P.O. BOX 13819 MILWAUKEE, WI 53213

Visit our web site for a complete listing of our titles with songlists.
www.halleonard.com

Prices and availability subject to change without notice.
Some products may not be available outside the U.S.A.

090